A *History of Disappearance*

A History of Disappearance

Poems by

Marjorie Stelmach

UNIVERSITY OF TAMPA PRESS
TAMPA, FLORIDA

Manufactured in the United States of America
Printed on acid-free paper ∞
First Edition

The University of Tampa Press
401 West Kennedy Boulevard
Tampa, FL 33606

ISBN 1-59732-008-0 ISBN 978-159732-008-5 (hbk.)
ISBN 1-59732-009-9 ISBN 978-159732-009-2 (pbk.)

Browse & order online at
http://utpress.ut.edu

Library of Congress Cataloging-in-Publication Data

Stelmach, Marjorie.
   A history of disappearance : poems / by Marjorie Stelmach. – 1st ed.
      p. cm.
   ISBN-13: 978-1-59732-008-5 (acid-free paper) ISBN-10: 1-59732-008-0 (acid-free paper)
   ISBN-13: 978-1-59732-009-2 (pbk. : acid-free paper) ISBN-10: 1-59732-009-9 (pbk. : acid-free paper)
   1. Loss (Psychology)–Poetry. 2. Grief–Poetry. I. Title.
   PS3569.T3798H57 2006
   811'.6–dc22   2006010993

Contents

i.

A History of Disappearance • 3
Radium • 4
Baptism • 8
The Underside • 9
The Skin of Your Mother's Eyes • 11
Graduation • 13
In this shot • 14
In a Finite Atmosphere • 15
Duplicity in the Telling • 17
A heart • 19

ii.

Chestnuts • 23
At the Czech Border • 25
Berlin: Spring Equinox • 27
These Hands Only • 30
Miniature: On the Irish Ferry • 32
Deathbed Confession • 33
Something Was Eating the House • 35
The Middle Spaces • 37
Back East • 39
Outside of That, The Whole • 41
The Tower • 44

iii.

Preservation • 55
Misaligned • 56
Floodfields & Fingerbones • 57
The Given • 60
Diseases of the Night • 61
As If the Dark Were a Wind • 66
Autumn • 68
Sleepwalk • 69
Presence • 70

iv.

Couplets for the Color Gold • 85
Spills • 86
What Cannot Be Summoned • 88
Mother of Lapse • 89
Ste. Thérèsa's Small Wrist • 94
Good Friday: On the Irish Coast • 96
...and are heavy laden • 100
The Consistency of the Human • 101
Sacred Waters • 103

v.

Invisible • 109
Splendor • 111
Faith and the Heavy Machinery • 113
Manna • 114
Poem in Which Krishna Appears As Heron • 116
Sunburn Song • 119
Tourist • 125
Autumnal • 127
Prayer • 128

Notes • 133
Acknowledgments • 135
About the Author and Artist • 137
About the Book • 139

In memory of my mother, Janet Scovill Herweg,
for my parents, John and Dorothy Herweg,
and, always, for Dan.

i.

What do you think love is, anyway?
I'll tell you, a harrowing.

—Mona Van Duyn

A History of Disappearance

In the rooms of our childhood, bowls of angelfish
    opened and closed like watery blooms,
        watching our lives pass.

When a headlight sliced the window glass,
    they rose like domestic moons, and briefly
        their mottled occupants entered

our dreams—cloud-eyed, wearing the O-gape
    of a wisdom shaped by water.
        As they turned

impassive faces on us, our shallow breathing broke
    and realigned in sync with the weak,
        hypnotic lift of gills. We woke

mistrustful. Increasingly, we imagined lapses:
    alchemies of shading, disquieting
        shifts of size,

an odd impermanence of marking. Nothing
    we could put a name to. After a time
        we were grown.

Radium

*Einstein said of Marie Curie that she had a soul
". . . poor, when it comes to the art of joy and pain."*

Liquids coil from darkness into beakers;
bright curls of metal
lace a foreground of gauges
                              and glass.
In white bodice and long, dark skirt,
Marie Curie waits for the flash,
fingers linked, eyes clear, insistence
in her lower lip.
                    Pierre
stands slightly back, behind
precise cylindrical weights;
formal coat; folded hands;
their dark, Parisian lab
                    about to glow.
Like Europe, then.
Like the century.

Half the century passed. In her portrait,
clipped from an old text and hung above my bed,
she wore her hair pulled back.
                              That year,
I combed my own curls out, unfolding them
from bobby pins, thin and tortured,
wiring all directions.
                    On good days,
mother let us play physician in her lab coat,
sing into her stethoscope, take crayons
to old X-ray film;
          wax flowers
          blossoming a black chest cavity;
          forests unfolding over a child's

winged scapula;
a bright lightning streak
                through an anklebone.

Winter came, its absences:
a different wing of the hospital, a numbered room,
the X-rays now her own.
                I pictured my mother's bones,
glowing; small buttons on her coat, showing
prim and clear against the spine; her lungs
like purses, filling, filling.
                She told us
they could see *us* in her heart. I knew
her breasts were gone.

She must have loved the keeping of the records—
                the alpha, beta, gamma *of it all;*
the scaled feel of the metal tubing, beakers
lifted into light,
the purification in cast-iron pots
of radium drawn from stone;
                loved, too,
the measured shadows of her woodshed lab,
leaky roof, no floor at all;
                loved even
the pacing in the freezing afternoons,
calming the child, while, at her touch, the elements
grew—transformed.
                That winter she lost fifteen pounds,
isolated radium, began
the dying. In later photographs,
the skin around her eyes looks
scarred.

Above my desk, my mother
                    in a long, dark coat
winces at the flash. I feel the current
every time I look.
          Home, that winter,
was a curtained hush. Mornings
I'd descend to breakfast counting breaths,
fingers calm on the banister.
                              Nights
were harder.
Currents ran my arms. Light
flooded my bones. My skin some nights
could ionize the air. I was sure
I was dying.

                    The fact
of laboratory cold.   *The myth*
of Radium.   .

                    The myth
of motherhood.   *The fact*
of Radium.

                    The fact
of motherhood.   *The myth*
of laboratory cold.

                    Madame Curie
died
of Radium,   *a fact*
                    it took a century to learn.

I watched her thin before my eyes that winter I was ten;
recall the tightening of her lips, the narrowing
of that long, dark coat;
                    cannot forget

a film of silvered lightning glimpsed
one awful day across her chest.

Pierre died first, crushed by a horse-drawn cart.
I wondered why she didn't die of that.
                        For years
I half-believed she died
of that same flash that placed her on my wall, died
of the myth,
                but no.
She died of her own elements:
                        time;
                        the pacing; laboratory cold;
                the practiced art of gathering impurities
                from stone.

It was joy
she died of—the work, the life—
                a bright,
painful scarring
about the breasts and eyes.

Baptism

This is the weather of her death,
the thunder's aftermath, the breath
before the next vertical light. This is the tenor
of the night we were first washed
in the world's weather:
                            a leaden dusk
into which the trees withdraw,
tossing resistance, leaning a deeper
compliance, removing themselves into the dual
necessity of the given—which is, and was,
the weather of her death.

Morning slipped over the ledge, as decorous as ever,
onto breakfast settings of silver and sugar,
her napkin ring, her chair—it was
like touching tissue paper, that air, that light,
that knowledge, unacknowledged.
                              We took up
simplicities—pleases and thank-yous
—but bodiless. He did not come down,
not even when we passed, complicit,
over the moment of grace. No one
came down
              to send us to school. Wordless,
we sleeved each other's jackets, took
our usual path. Only at the playground steps
did we see what silence had fallen on us.
Acorns pebbled the cement, strewn by storm
and cracking now underfoot
like tiny thunder.
                      In our separate classrooms
we learned what we were asked, while
in our absence, a long morning sun
fell bare on the cleared table.

The Underside

Solstice, summer's longest stitch.
Light edging down aslant on the lake
where lily pads lie, doubled back on themselves,
their veined, mauve undersides splayed beneath
the green, encroaching evening.
Sun departing, slow
as a rich uncle from the old days,
out on the screened porch, talking,
his broad hat passing hand to hand,
weight shifting, leaning against
the doorjamb, then the window ledge,
on and on in a broadening shade.
The door at his back, almost unbearable
in glare, and beyond, the splinter-lit steps
to the sidewalk we'd all be following soon
toward fins, white chrome, and a trailered boat.

Where am I in this scene? Who is this man? This uncle,
whose jowls distort my view of his eyes, whose hatless hand
roams my hair as it darkens from warm gold and dulls,
while over and over he doesn't leave — but surely must,
already he's shaken my father's hand, embraced my mother,
kissing the air close to her mouth like funeral kin —
but stays, beginning one more story,
slow from his wide mouth and tasty in his eyes,
the one about the guy who'd never fished,
had brought along a grappling hook in case . . . ; this uncle,
this man with gear and a boat grappled to his car,
rumbling on of rods and lures, of costly nets and a creel
large enough for Lake Superior trout; this sportsman, bound
for the Upper Peninsula's tip, where his golf club
served us dinner once, and drinks in stemmed glassware;
who claims to remember my sipping, the face I made . . . ;
who says he has only stopped to see

how we are, all these long years;
this long long day, this endless lingering
of a hand that, by the end, had taken all the gold I had,
this fallen face that has stayed
for decades, nameless in my memory,
though I know that his boat was the *Lucky Catch*
and that something so lengthy was happening all around
it isn't over yet.

The Skin of Your Mother's Eyes

All that day we'd been ranging our space, grown wider over winter,
   finding each other again, all of us taller, tougher.

What brought me home that afternoon? Something
   about the house, wrong—drapes pulled midday, a stilled

and darkened air. Quietly crossing to where she lay, I imagined her
   drifting off: the slight stir of the fan's blades,

the lift of lilac and cut grass, our calls and spilling laughter falling
   like lassoes over the neighborhood lawns. Or had she fallen

so fast, so deep, she heard nothing after the slam of the screen,
   and nothing still as I circled the couch, imagining: *dying.*

Did she lie there wondering what was best: to capture and tickle to tears
   this daughter? to circle her round, laughing, and hold her—

a mother's small strength against the serious words of a father?
   Or best to let me begin it, the coming to terms

that must include the grotesque and dramatic, as well as the nights
   of staring straight up at mute loss, learning

the accurate words for it. Even today, I can't let it go, reliving,
   revising the scene between us: she, in a deep,

or feigned, sleep; I, in my scarred, white knees, returning
   again and again to that dim living room to renew my renewable tears.

It's a terrible blindness we come from; another we come *to* at the end.
   That, or a terrible courage. I can't say which

[11]

or what such a choice might mean. Her eyelids were skin.
 I had not, I think, known that before about eyes. Skin, but pale

and veined as petals fallen to the carpet from a white poinsettia.
 Or leaves from inside pistachio shells, those frail inner papers.

Or thin tissues of watered clay? Or softly creased Easter-glove leather?
 What names can you find for the skin of your mother's eyes?

Why do the words, even now, matter? And when is the task over?

Graduation

That September hopscotch squares were painted
blinding white. For weeks we crushed a breed
of white-capped acorns underfoot. Inside,
gold leaves
bordered the chalkboard. Our desks were bolted
into line, our names Scotch-taped.

By spring the chipped lines let us cheat,
dancing, stomping, hissing names at one another's backs.
By then the board had gone through skeletons,
snowmen, sleighs; we'd learned to slump
and reach the desk in front of us
with our muddy feet.

By the time she died, we'd tacked up spring:
tulips, daises—simple symmetrical shapes. At recess,
only the scuffed remains of an old white. Released,
we turned to the chase. For a time there was blood
to be bandaged: graveled knees,
the scraped heels of palms.

June came down—the boards now bare,
except for tacks and scraps of old construction paper.
With early heat to keep us shaded in the far field,
we quieted, played counting games with stones
among the cool roots. One day,
not one of us was crying.

In this shot

the metallic glint of pipe on the right
was the angular rise of the swing set.

That semi-circular shadow there in the foreground
fell from the merry-go-round.

The scatter of acorns, looking like flaws in the print?
It was autumn; they were everywhere, crushed underfoot.

The sky would have hurt your eyes
with blue, I suppose, if this weren't black and white,

and the chipped paint of the hop-scotch squares
would have shot out the amber of caution.

The blood stains, though, are gone,
soaked into the grain or washed to the creek,

or perhaps they had not fallen yet
on the pocked concrete.

I was awfully small at the time it was taken; still,
the single footprint may well have been mine,

and if I look closely enough, a face
may rise from the glossy finish, just

as the murderer's does, reversed,
in the victim's eyes.

In a Finite Atmosphere

One of those ungraspable truths: that it's all still here,
    each atom of every exhalation, each breath drawn on earth
      and released.

In illustrations it takes the name of Jesus or Galileo.
    Homer. Joan of Arc. *Just think*, they say. I do:
      I breathe statistics,

and the face of the Shepherd appears; the fine anklebones
    of Achilles; the lifted palm, bowed legs
      of Gandhi, the ears.

But it's far too easy. These days, like Psyche at her seeds,
    I've returned to the task of the earning back
      of love; to the skills

of sift and separation, of industry and attention.
    In the long years of labor to come, I'll learn to part
      the particled air,

to reconvene her singular breath, torn those last years
    in pain and fury and fear, but always
      in astonishment

from the Great Air—some tendrils lost in ocean depths,
    some scattering the sand of the far dunes,
      some deep in earth's gilded shafts,

some here. Some surely here. *Mother,*
    I made you a promise once, which I renew.
    I'll hold my breath till I turn blue

with you, sky-colored at last; hold fast for the rest of my life —
not long, I know; exhale in death
what it is I can't, alive, recall:

the dusty light on your calm face,
the narrow tendons of your heel, your hand
on my hair,

your bowed and beautiful bones.

Duplicity in the Telling

Be wary of ellipsis, the dotted cut-line
of the inessential. Remain alert to the false

cord of concision, the attendant narrowing,
the treacherous, long drawing out.

Take special care to distinguish their voices.
Remind yourself they have come to sound

identical in your dreams because
how else would you listen?

There was a house once, you might begin.
Snows came to the yard for the twin sleds,

trees bled sap solely for the smell of it on your palms
those nights you slept courageously in the high fort.

This is before. Everyone's young. The light
slants thick on all that's left of the old

linoleum, ladder-back chairs, stars of spilt sugar.
The tiniest grains cast outsized shadows.

Still, you might be forgiven a bit
of reticence: some things *are* understood.

It may not prove essential to mention
the child's bed in the living room, railed

against a restlessness—and later, pain. Accuracy
is hard, costly; this was, after all, a lifetime ago.

Two lifetimes ago. Be vigilant, too, concerning
the similar faces, only one of them a child's.

Resist duplicity in the telling, the pull
of identical pulses: elide / be sparing of elision.

A heart

and an arrow drawn finger-fat
on a window pane
      steamy from steeping soup,
its filmy, risen tissues pressed
thinly on the glass to allow
          and erase
the children's messages to her—
transient, a winter lace.
      Above the coils, a woman
they're told has come
to mother them now
         sweeps a smile
across the space and returns
to the work.

      (On the far side
in the outer cold
a bird dips
     and lifts a small heart,
carving across the sky's slate
a curved departure
        that stays
and stays,
drawn by what,
    if not love?)

What if not love?

ii.

I have walked through many lives
some of them my own,
and I am not who I was. . . .

–Stanley Kunitz

Chestnuts

He offered me
a small white bag of roasted chestnuts.
It was raining, I remember;
the bag warmed my hands.
                I drew one out
and took it on my tongue without looking
away from his eyes. Sweet, dark—
like nothing I'd tasted.
                Above us,
the gargoyles of Notre Dame dripped
in leering imitation of the world's spring sorrows.
In the small garden, everything
was newly pruned
                and wet.
It's not as if I didn't know.
                They tasted
like—what? like softening roots,
like the smoke of his voice in my dream,
like him
in my arms all night.
                He offered me
their name in his own tongue.
Not *chestnuts*—
something with an M,
                and I wondered
what hums and sibilance rose
from the tongues that met that day
when the serpent let the woman understand
she would not die.
                Taste this
(sweet hiss from tongues of grinning
stone), *taste this, I promise
it won't be wrong.*

[23]

Our day, too,
hardly qualified as evil.
Paris. April. Only rain was falling
onto gates flung open
to busloads of tourists.

If gargoyles were crying,
well, they were gargoyles; they knew
their purpose.
Small and far below them,
vendors went on
offering the warm bitter fruit
of the chestnut,
selling the soft bite, the sudden waters
of our mouths.

I remember
the way they warmed my fingers in the rain,
promising the taste of sweetness
and the dark.

I, too, will try anything
once, pay anything. *Promise I won't die.*

At the Czech Border

That day the final snow was falling again in the mountain passes,
    cloud banks arrested by patterns of high and low pressure,
        spring detained at the border.

We crawled uphill past a line of trucks so long it would break
    the spirit of any century. Above us in shadowed cabs,
        drivers dozed at wheels designed

to tilt to the twelve positions sufficient to any man's needs;
    others clustered in scuffed snow,
        exchanging talk that must last all night,

must stall and hover, explaining everything over and over,
    when, in the end, it would all come down again
        to the unendurable.

Mile after mile of men preparing to step out of line,
    to beckon the one woman forward. . . because
        there were women, and had been for miles.

How to speak of their silent company, trudging the shoulder,
    lining our way up the mountain.
        Or standing, ghostly, in falling snow,

their faces painted to cross the distance to men
    in their endless lines,
        in their always surprising *need*.

How to describe the accumulation of mismatch: wet snow
    on uncovered hair; heeled boots
        on the rough embankment.

How to account for the way it gathered too slowly in me,
   the knowledge of why. Twilight. We offered up
      our passports—no questions, no goods to declare.

Descending, we watched our headlights fold on cliff faces,
   fall over edges. Above, in unreachable lands
      where spring would pass its one more night,

the highest peaks shot light across the darkening territories;
   higher still, the falling stones of the zodiac fell
      into their old places,

as women and men passed undocumented into one night
   in the world, and the silence between us
      entered its new language.

Berlin: Spring Equinox

All evening
a light snow fell at the glass,
shifting at intervals into ice.
        In the mirror a parallel fall of light
ticked over the sheets,
over his face.
        Around us,
Berlin seemed to raise its monuments
into the sky on tissues of white, weightless
as history.
        Strangers above us, below us,
passed through their numbered doors,
crossed into
        and out of their dreams,
or talked softly together,
                Babel
rising again after forty years
of what we would learn to call the long
misapprehension.

That night, History
entered my dream, a misstep:

        a young man (his father? my father?)
        called to the war, returns damaged —
        returns to Berlin,
        to forty years of learning his crutches,
        until he can move through our midst again
        entirely silent and touchingly
                        graceful.

On the far edge of the dream,
a plane turned on a runway — my plane?

waking me to a sudden
certainty—*too late.*
        And yes, while we slept,
Europe's clocks had advanced one hour in an instant,
refolding the tissues of light above us.

As I packed my belongings, soft globes of snow
passed over my face in the mirror, while ice
struck the glass at my back,
                                        Berlin
a full degree colder somehow
than its own reflection,
a lapse—
like grace descending crippled,
or history's heartfelt apology,
                                        late.

As he drove, I drifted back into the dream
where Time's broken body was lifted
and lowered
        into a future where we would agree
to call the light by its new name.

Out on the icy runway
my plane was already turning.
Around us, monuments went on rising
into the swirling sky,
                                and soon,
his voice would promise
a future, would promise
to love me forever.

In this way, Love
entered the dream, a misstep.

Love: the practiced grace of the broken;
the distance
        lifting between us; the whole
                impossible world.
What we have agreed to call *the world.*
The world.

These Hands Only

Debris lines the spiritless lick along the Italian coast
               where she strides the Private Beaches.
For as far as she can see, there is nothing;
             even the ocean is nearly soundless.
Ashore, there's only dead air and the stir
          of a languorous worker here and there
             at the shut resorts.
They clutch their crotches as she passes.
Their mouths open at her back,
             crying *Bella.*

Out of the hazy distance a sulky grows,
             its driver muffled to the eyes in a slicker.
The horse's tongue, pinkly immense, hangs
         from the side of its mouth's black gap,
spoiling the landscape for miles.
       She slows to watch them weave and plow
             the various depths of the surf's break
for the tests they offer of roar and fear, of swerve
and the sudden cut: the work of learning
           these hands only.

ii.
A man is dragging an altar block down
       from Carrara's white slopes
to the circular saws of Pietrasanta,
       a master of marble, whose hands
were born to the work, whose diamond teeth
       must turn beneath a continuous fall
of water—or the blades will burn; such men
       have worked this stone forever.
The dream, too, takes place under water.

iii.
On the flight home, her ears are bothered by pressure.
  Mouths move around her; she can't speak
the language. Below, the Alps are a string of white skulls
    that a hard morning sun sets alight, but can't soften.
Crossing such sternness unnerves her: the unaccountable
    swerves and lurches. The peaks are substantially
higher now. In the seats around her, passengers stir
    and seem to take on a more literal flesh. A sudden
vacuum and catch—one more such jolt and, she knows,
    they'll drop from the sky. What happens next

will seem to happen under water. Those who escape
    immediate death will emerge form scorched metal
into a deep, unreachable cut; white rock will mark
    the site where they'll die—or eat flesh.
She'll be the first one eaten; she hasn't learned the words
    to plead for her life. Mouths will open around her,
deciding: *Bella.* She'll be so easily taken: *these hands only.*

Miniature: On the Irish Ferry

The wake presses its root into black
waters, a soil
        where nothing holds.
Ireland almost erased,
     and the moon rising
to assume her place, inert above
the steady drone
        of engines moving
            over cold.

Our hands bone-white on the rail, we watch
for a long time.
       Later, the sky
will force God upon us: the moon
striking a hazed cross,
         undeniable;
cloud-tissues, starred
and sheeting over so balanced a crossbeam,
we can't escape what we see—nails,
      and the meaning
          of nails.

Reduced to our flesh, unable to speak
of our parting
     or what the sky has shown us,
        we stand, untouching,
under the moon, above the drone.
Small.
And every moment,
     everything
growing smaller
around us.

Deathbed Confession

All I got was a message from Wetherell saying,
"Can you make me a monster?"
   –Christian Spurling, inventor of the Loch Ness Monster

Waking nameless in a grey
                    rolled light,
on a bed bolted to a wall in the hold
of a ship off England's southern coast,
         strangely queasy,
memory lost,
         I felt the moment stretch and touch
the edge of terror before,
across the cabin his shape emerged
         from uniform gloom,
                    and one by one,
the shapes we'd gathered there:
         the Irish whiskey; two plastic cups;
         an open suitcase;
                    somewhere in the list,
                              my life.

All of which comes back this morning
as *her* shape rises from newsprint dots,
                    floating
in the famous gloom
         of 1934 Loch Ness,
                    above her, the headline
we knew would come:
         Loch Ness Monster A Fraud
         Inventor Confesses

Another deathbed truth, the millions of them
         rising from our lives
         like light from dead stars,

and, by this world's measure,
no great loss, except
it's nothing now, the Loch
that once was hers:
                                empty as the lives
we rise into some mornings,
waking to a queasiness,
                afraid, almost,
to wonder who we are in this immortal dark;
who it was first made us up,
                at whose request;
                whose fraud,
the lives we lift into this world,
                the emptiness we lift them from.

Something Was Eating the House

Something multiple, rhythmic,
unceasing. Not wings. Not the rubbing
of legs. Whatever it was, its name
was legion.

      We never mentioned it to our hosts, but
discreetly we searched the rafters at bedtime;
mornings we checked the floorboards for sawdust—
no trace.

      And still, as each dark fell, the growl
would begin above us, the *gritting / grinding /
scraping / abrading*. We worked toward the word,
the exact description:

             butterflies,
             millions of butterflies,
                   gritting their teeth;
             gravel-gulleted mice, swallowing,
             swallowing;
                swallows, grinding and eating
                their own bones;
             bats, their nightmare hearts beating
             like seeds.

We slept fitfully. Night after night,
a hot wind up from Africa lifted the dust,
carried it, laid it again
to the North.

      The water shortage grew acute;
sunflowers and the sheep suffered; even the stones
reflected it down from the steep village. The birds
stopped singing.

Their eldest son was murdered at Heathrow, we heard,
the following Christmas,
a simple, gratuitous violence.

      I imagine this grief come upon them—

the fine lines near her eyes, deepened;
his limp, minutely increased—
                              and recall
how we washed in as little water as possible
those three weeks, wanting then
to be faithful, return what we could to our hosts
for the generous days of that summer.
                              But nights,
I remember lying mute,
while something relentless ate that house.

The Middle Spaces

Years away from India, without warning, the dreams began:
    human landscapes sifting down to the banks
        of the Ganges.

Women, somnambulistic, self-contained, gracefully lifting
    layers of cloth to uncover and cleanse one portion
        of flesh at a time

and lowering them again in smooth, unbroken motions,
    offering no glimpse of skin; stricken creatures
        moving their pain

down the lapped steps; solemn mourners bearing the wrapped
    flesh of their dead down to the proper place
        for the burning,

knowing where, knowing how, the elements
    of eternity would descend to take these human
        briefnesses back.

Daily she'd stand on the banks above, awed by the ritual
    foldings and unfoldings; daily she'd watch the dead rise,
        flesh and ghost

above the river. At times an arm, cords tightened by
    intensity of heat, would lift into the middle spaces,
        an eloquent gesture, lost

between the long wash of the human below, and above,
    the slow unending stream of gods.
        In the shallows

dogs quarreled over bits of human flesh; only the women
in their slow dance kept faith with beauty.
For years she kept

her distance, painting the perfect squares and curves
of Buddhist monasteries, their dim interiors,
the geometric casts

of light on the rich mahoganies. Then, older
and a world away, without warning—
the dreams.

On canvas after canvas now she paints the draped dead
of Benares, roped for immolation at the edge
of the Ganges.

In each, a single wrapped form floats in the unmarked space
where two dimensions keep the artist's faith
with three:

a purified earth; an air burned white; and between,
the things we do to one another's flesh
that we call grief.

Beneath the plaincloth, bound and borne to the stretched surface,
we recognize the shape of something shaped
like us.

Nearby: a broken loaf of bread, a few uneven stones,
and often, unaccountably, a small,
carved box.

Back East

Out West, where thunder roughens the borders
of national parks, the Natives toss
in unsettling dreams
of treaties being hammered out.
        Or it could be the bikers
in the motel lot, their leather wrists breaking
against my breath, as they plot
my abduction down miles of bad road
through the Reservations—
me astride, holding hard, no reverse.
        They've offered
America again—all of it, everything,
revving their Harleys all night
outside the Best Western.
        But I'm waiting for another,
waiting back East in a waste of dream,
half-waking to the sounds of household motors
turning themselves on—
an unraveling hum I turn back
into rain from the mountains.
        Soon after moonset,
I open my length to the spine of Death,
a helmeted sculptor who's come for me
on a quiet machine,
        a BMW R1100,
engineered to perfection in black—
black gloves, black boots, and hands
that, till now, have worked only
the fine-grained granite of the Old World.
        He's come for America's
underside, for eternity's opposite number—erosion.
Together we'll tour the Parklands, racing
between canyon walls at whose base

pale petals flash past—*datura,*
the deathly, delicate colors
of marble, and equally captive of light.
                              But fragile. They'll crush
like American flesh from the East caught white
in a motel mirror.
            At dawn, in my nightgown, down in the lot,
I'll kneel and confess and confess and confess,
my chilled hands pressed to the cylinder grilles
of the spurned Harley drivers,
enduring the third-degree burns that alone
might assuage this unspeakable cold.
                        But I still can't go with them.

Back East, in my bones, in my dreams, I go on
rehearsing the one
wild ride I'll deny for the rest of my life.
                              At dawn
I awaken imagining wind on my visor, an ache
in my lower back as I bend
to bear nothing forward into the Old
Frontier, embracing only the Sun in his blinding white
helmet, its bright acrylic smeared with wings
and the blood of those insignificant lives we erase
by our simplest forward motion.

Outside of That, The Whole

for Thomas Kinsella

You write of the stars' mathematical crawl across your glass,
and of course it's the same in my own Midwest,
stars being constant.
                    In all that summer
I entered Dublin only once, near nightfall,
not a single star.
                    Outside of that, the whole of Ireland
filled the need I'd lately felt
to let it all go, to sip and tell the old tales only
to the wail and drone of only the oldest instruments,
the pipes and concertinas.
                    I recall one street brawl
in a coastal town that bubbled on for hours,
while I lay listening above, smeared
by neon's off and on.
                    In the pub next day
I looked hard: only the one
black eye.

But that summer it didn't take long
to give up breaking things down along obvious lines
in search of some bent revelation, the rainbow-remains
of a promise.
                    Then one evening for a single hour,
I knelt in a dusk-lit, Dublin church,
gazing up at a cut-glass virgin—dolphin-curved, lovely,
lighter than light—and a coterie of lean young martyrs,
who hovered close in blues, golds, and startling
crimsons.
                    Below, slim candles
lengthened a central elongated arch,

from within which a tall son of God looked on,
smiling, collecting white light,
                            and blessing,
blessing, while a dim rainbow of stained sun fell
through the glass to crease on the white
stone floor. A single hour.
                            Outside of that,
the whole lost summer.

No real evidence; still I'm convinced
from that same glassworks came your cool glass,
an old-world pane through which you watched
the blurred, retreating galaxies
cast light like ancient insults over
our glossiest designs,
                            designs being constant,
time short, and stars always crawling off
toward what's outside the frame.
No choice in this; they can't reverse—
though for all we know in the vast vastness
they'll curve
                            and, well outside our lives,
will be back around.

I wonder if you, too, crossed the world
to let things go,
hoping to find in a new green land
nothing to own up to,
                            no wounds or songs, nothing
to love or shrug off,
as you took up old habits of watchfulness,
gazing out through our new-world glass

(source unknown, and cut
                    to a universal fit)
into that square of escaping stars.
And, outside of that,
                    the whole.

The Tower

For the soul is a strangeness on the earth.
                              −Georg Trakl

I. From the Parapet

I have heard the demons howling in my blood.
                              −Georg Trakl

Four hundred stone steps to the parapet;
 three hundred and sixty ways to fall:
  one way to see it.

Far below, Siena coils
 from the Campo core, where swarms
  of tourists confirm the simple

equations of human reduction.
 Up here, a steady wind assaults us,
  producing an equal and opposite force,

a bodily readjustment that leaves us
 leaning out over the rail
  to take in the spiral of walls, the curve

of the countryside, earth's rounded drop—
 all matched to the ear's own intricate coil.
  We shout to be heard,

our words unequal to the blood's roar:
 lean a bit more, nothing to stop you,
  look straight down at it: death.

We look straight down at the bleached bricks,

where the tower's shadow shrinks
toward noon.

Twin rows of skulls whiten our grip.
Suppose this wind stopped abruptly . . .
Abruptly, the hour strikes;

eleven murderous blows fall on the Campo.
Stillness spreads like an echo,
all of us counting,

as if not merely the hour but the age itself
were in doubt. As if, like Galileo,
we, too, were imprisoned here,

silenced like him against the peril
of all we could prove: an ever-increasing
error in the pace of things;

the unspeakable equality of falling.

II. The Descent

*Tell me I must have the strength to stay alive and to do
what is true. Tell me that I am not mad.*

—Georg Trakl

Down. The strange hard work of climbing down
    past the huge bell, silent now
        unless you count words—

a suicide message scratched in the lip:
    from this point we die. A pen or knife
        returned, then, to a dark pocket,

and only the weight of their bodies left. Their flight.
    And the aftermath of official hands
        sifting for names and a reason—

the infamous *sharp object* of death.
    One flight down, a second message
        carved on a stone window ledge: two names

and a line of Italian in which I can read
    the one word *love.*
        Love makes me pause.

Did they hold each other, jump face to face?
    Did they join hands, fall forward like swallows?
        Or leap *up*, exultant? And

why does it matter? More than matter,
    the only thing this moment in all the hard world
        the matters? And why

does it cease to matter and let me go down?

III. Solid Ground

We fall into an inapprehensible darkness. How could dying,
the moment which leads to eternity, ever be short?

—Georg Trakl

Below, on the warm slant of the Campo,
    the tower's shadow recedes beneath
        a sunburned couple at rest in its shade.

Ankles crossed, eyes closed, they're poised unaware
    at the crown's cast edge. Abruptly,
        their blonde hair blazes.

Haloed like Giotto's holy people,
    one straightened arm afire behind them,
        they're lifted by light from the parapet.

Only their long crossed legs
    remain in the shade. They appear
        to be falling, and the tower goes on

withdrawing its dark support at a rate
    equal to everything else. *From this point we die.*
    Light fills their sunburnt faces

as they float mid-air, and it's all clear:
    two ways to die
        on the same stone ground.

One way to see it.

IV. Song of the West

. . . to give to the truth what belongs to the truth.

          –Georg Trakl

Back on my accustomed bench in Casole D'Elsa,
    my tired legs stretched in the sun, I read
        from Trakl's *Song of the West*

and tell myself it's an accident, all this death.
    Trakl's wish: *to give to the truth*
        what belongs to the truth.

That, and to die.
    His sister, they say, was his only love,
        her fingers moving on ivory keys

in his earliest dreams of bone;
    moving a little later down
        his shivering spine. Always

the two of them, bearing their truth
    like beauty's mark, *eyeing each other,*
        trembling, waking again and again

from identical dreams, landscapes
    filled with the broken spines
        of thoroughbreds; brother and sister

filling their blood with drugs they prayed
    would bring them escape—from
        love, from each other. But

war came first. One day he watched
    a human brain spread itself on a wall,
        and fleeing, found corpses strung

from trees outside the hospital tents.
No drugs. No dream.
          A *stony darkness*, he wrote,

has broken upon me. I try, like him,
     to look straight at it, but here
          at the century's end,

from this walled city high above fields
     of sunflowers turned in the waning day
          toward the West, his words

draw me deeper into the shadows
     where truth remains *unsäglich*.
          Unspeakable:

two ways to see it.

V. A Love Song

My work is an all too faithful mirror of a godless, accursed century.

–Georg Trakl

From the hills around this high stone city, bells
    call sheepdogs back to the fierce work
        of herding:

a fury of muscle and teeth, met
    with an always-bewildered, bleating grief.
        Daily, the same assault, the same

befuddled misery, never softened over the years
    into ceremony, never over the ages
        finally unnecessary.

From a high window a tenor sings—or a tape—
    a love song, at least, and sung only once,
        the world allowing belief.

And for now, winding back through the single street
    with the fresh fruit and kilo of bread
        I'll eat after dark,

I want more to live than I want to die.
    Perhaps it's the simple supper,
        the fall of light

onto swallows' wings, or the sound of opera
    off in the hills. Or perhaps it's the peace
        I've come to of late,

falling free from a shortening life, or
    drifting back effortlessly
        into light.

From the walls, I watch tiny sheep
    urged homeward, all detail lost.
        The radiant, closing sunflowers cast

spoked shadows into the dust,
    their darkness advancing like ancient armies
        of the saddened and ceremonious.

In their wake, I'll move to my bread and wine,
    to sleep, to the rest of my life, which may be
        so little: that truth,

and my finite number of ways to see it.

iii.

down here, between
one solitude and the next, love comes
to this, to nothing but this.

–Donald Finkel

Preservation

At dawn the Tuscan skies drape birdsong over
    new-made bales of hay, the walls
        of high, stone cities. Distance hides

in folds of hills and mist. Wings lift and dip;
    grapes ripen in their ballerina rows,
        rising toward a wine that vows

to leave no after-aches—no matter
    the quantity you drink or the pain you bring
        to the long night of drinking.

No preservatives, my host explains. *No need.*
    In Tuscany, time leaks. Noon
        is leaking as we speak.

Buona sera, the men say now from the sidewalk tables.
    Bells draw families home to long-drawn meals:
        fresh apricots, a fine Chianti.

✦

I waken worlds away from Tuscany,
    rising from twisted sheets with a headful of regret
        for the preservative weakness of the local wine,

my eyes lifting to brick, straining for a sign
    that wings have passed; but only the clock
        carries us on

into the long afternoon, when high in our offices we pause
    and sigh, wondering what it is we're listening for—
        something we know should be happening now

—a *buona sera,* a bell.

Misaligned

Tonight as your rain lifts, across the world mine falls.
Only the stars appear to us both unmoved.

Take one molecule of distance, you have
a prayer already. We're composed of such crushed

emptiness. Of secrets, too. Secrets kept
for no remembered reason, as we keep our bones

inside us, holding our hands to the light
simply to watch them lie beneath the skin like old gods

under ice. Secrets colorless as tapers on the altar
of the chapel of Our Lady, where later I'll go

to bathe my own secret bones in a stained light
and breathe the suspended dust, puffed

from a kneeler's cushion where someone rising, sighing,
left behind two indentations, aligned.

In the world, somewhere, the rain.

Floodfields & Fingerbones

Bridges loosen at their roots, levees buckle,
    the current snaps off in the middle
    of the telecast pastor
        of the New Life Baptist Church.
No candles in the house.

In your dim cathedral across the world,
    candles abound.
    You burn them in your letters,
        thin and white as fingerbones,
praying my safety.

> *In Chartres*
> *we lit two candles, sealed them,*
> *made one flame.*
>   *That night*
> *our fingers seared all we could touch*
> *of one another's flesh, left marks*
> *that burned for hours.*
>   *It was all we could do*
> *to prevent the healing, all we could carry*
> *when we escaped inland.*

On *Late Night News*, the moon breaks
    and spills into our yards,
    climbs onto our porches, reaches
        into bureau drawers
and mirrors.

And expert blames a Philippine volcano,
    ashes blown across the stars.
    This hour's lead: *The Tragedy of the Dead,*
        how they're rising in their coffins,
dry as bones.

[57]

If forced to evacuate (the knock on the door
    in the middle of the night),
    what will I take?
        My rooms look back at me.
They know I don't love them

enough to save them. Water.
    I'll take water, all the water I can carry.
    And your letters, their cathedrals,
        smoke rising from your fingers—
safety safety safety.

> *Fingerbones of moonlight fell*
> *like ashes on my face. I was running*
> *across waters, carrying what I could*
> *up the ramp of an excursion boat*
> *plying the Missouri.*
> > *Slow that night,*
> *the river. We drowsed and watched the last*
> *of the night birds settle,*
> *until the guide's voice woke us:* Ladies and Gents,
> coming up on your left, a petrified fall.
> > *A hundred of us moved as one to port.*
> *When we capsized, I was holding*
> *water in my arms.*
> *Water alms. An offering: blankets*
> *for the drowned.*
> > *I woke to water*
> *running over my face,*
> *hard as cathedral wax, light*
> *as pumice stone,*
> > *and I knew*
> *I'd not been touched in a long long time.*

The waters on my screen peel
        slate and white in turns,
        a run of the moon over floodfields and ruins.
            On screen, the flood is made of light:
light made of candles; candles made of—what?

Of bees? fingerbones?
        the ashes of your letters blown across the stars?
        The New Life pastor may be right,
            we're in God's hands, but
it's not the same as safety.

Hard days ahead
        of looting and film crews;
        of moonfingers tangling the hair of the dead,
            who are already dressed
for this service and need

only rescue;
        of searching for the stranded,
        who, I think, have not been touched
            by anyone this faithful
in a long long time.

As for me,
        I'll escape inland again. Carry what I can.
        Light a candle for me in your distant cathedral.
            Tonight, I need
what the dead need.

The Given

Late winter rain dents the crust, erodes the ice.
Acidic pools widen, a lacework spread over
the earth, embedded
                        with avid birds seduced
as always by the first
hard, green sun.

Crushed patches of grass surface,
the color of warts, and the worst of it is
spring's so far off,
                        I can't envision
even your eyes—green? brown?
—with conviction.

The forecast calls for freeze, more snow,
a week of below-zero chill. I can see it now:
these deluded birds,
                        worm-driven,
sealed over in their stupid glee
by a cellophane wind.

Need is a fool's prediction. Witness
these singing multitudes silenced
in a shrink-wrapped spring,
                        while cosmic weights
slide back and clamp into
their previous slots

and everything obedient to light
obediently dies.
I'll hedge my bets—it's safer
                        —and dream tonight
of the pure
slush-color of your eyes.

Diseases of the Night

I. The Disease of Watching

when the cause is known, it must be removed

It's this damned clock / faucet /
dusk-to-dawn light on the lawn / cat.
It's this inextinguishable
green square,
the after-image of the mirror,
afloat on my lids like one of Chagall's
green fiddlers.
           Mother played
when we were young—the pine-scent
of rosin, its thick translucence;
the indentation left in the soft
underflesh of her jaw.
           A long-legged insect
suspended in amber
rested against the white of her throat;
the soft narrow mouth of a fox
bit fox-fur at her shoulders, those nights
when she came to check on our sleep, late,
and the light from the hall caught her face
in the mirror.
           Back then, a window-fan
hummed all night
till she and Dad came home, and now
there's nothing. It's this
damned silence.

the irritated spirits must be appeased
with emulsions, especially of poppy seed,
or with other opiates in general

Behind the medicine-cabinet mirror,
we kept our secrets: cut-glass bottles
in iodine blue, mercurochrome red;
sleeping and stomach and headache powders;
swabs, cotton-gauze,
tape, tiny scissors;
razors and matches to sterilize needles.
Evidence of our tended cuts,
torn tissues. We understood
that only something stinging worse
would clean and cure us.
            My world's too gentle.
This comforter and pillow,
these deep-pile rugs. Uncauterized,
unsalved, I'm simply drugged—
on soft-plastic capsules.

   with old persons, the moderate use
   of generous wine may be allowed in the evening, likewise
   medicines of amber and musk will be proper

My only amber is the dusk-to-dawn—
sleepless guardian of my dark walk.
And musk? A perfume lost
to another time.
           As for the generosities
of a moderate wine, I can't yet bring myself
to drink alone.

   others recommend preparations of barley,
   emulsions of poppy-seeds, decoctions
   of scorzonera roots, almond-cream
   and winter flummery; tea made of cowslip-flowers

Sick-room smells: the abrasive pleasures
of plasters and broths, their pungencies
and stinks.
                    Nothing smells
in my whole house.
No honeysuckle off the sleeping porch,
no pine-stir in the wind,
no oniony supper smells drifting up
from the neighbors downstairs.
                    My sheets
smell of the laundry, I smell of nothing,
and you are gone.
Only the cat smells a bit of us. A bit
like we used to.

II. The Disease of the Incubus, or Night-Mare

*the incubus rarely seizes any one except
during sleep, especially if the patient lies on his back*

I thought at first
it was our old cat, come
to tap a paw on my shoulder
to be let out.
        Old cat, long in the grave
of an earlier house, old Marble,
I thought it was you.
At first.
Then I thought it was you,

> *those seized with it seem to have a heaviness on their breasts,
> and if they want to speak they cannot*

. . . and I couldn't breathe.
A tarred darkness, or the ceiling
come down, or the strong scent of pine
nailed inches above me. Time
drawn slowly into my lungs,
a terrible amber syrup, and I thought—
I thought I was young.

> *but after a long struggle: at length they awake,
> and the weight vanishes*

Maybe if I bury my face
in the pillow and imagine myself
sipping cowslip tea or
spooning winter flummery with our old cat,
this weight will vanish.
        Outside it's amber,
dusk to dawn. Almost as if
someone were watching.

but sometimes they find a tremor of the heart, remains.
there are some instances of its being mortal,
though it is generally without danger

Morning. And there's dawn to dusk
to get through now,
lugging around this foolish, leftover
tremor of the heart,
            which seems today
an unbearable burden, but which
may be only mortal.

As If the Dark Were a Wind

In the pressing darkness, the window glass
strains long and relents,
as if the dark were a wind. Listen.
A fluttering sound, a sound
like a shiver that might pass
down a widower's spine, his face
in his hands at the kitchen table, the tremble
of bones enclosed in the ill-
fitted socket of grief.
        They will tell you it's all
the wind's doing, these random caesuras
that let the glass settle a moment before
it's taken to stress-point again,
but I think it's the press
of the outer dark and the pane's
nightly longing to pass through the aperture
into a room full of warmth and light,
making a simple, invisible entry that no one
will notice until a gust comes at the gap
and cold sweeps down
requiring an explanation, and always
before you can speak: the white
of the gorgeous storm.

        We don't fit our place here
for long. The longing that brought us,
that longing will take us. Like a birth
or a death, it's no one's doing exactly—a weather
brought against walls not intended to hold,
intended to yield to a presence intent
upon moving into the world,
                  or out,
unaware of how huge
the loss of the previous life will seem,

and how soon;
unaware of the new longing to follow,
of how restrictive the space, any space, will become
over time in the eyes of the one who sought entry,
eyes that must open and know no entry
is less unforgiving than any other, no shelter
less gorgeous, less stormed.

Autumn

Soon again the dead will outnumber
the living. Last night the moon was fat. I dreamt
so many dreams, and all were death. I can't guess
where green goes. Sucked back under
the earth to brood and bear a brash, relentless crop
of weed and wing? Or into the sallow sky to drop
a pale green dusk or help a wan sun rise again,
a sickly dawn?

          And what a wilderness to mourn in:
curbs lined with the rotting dead; this wailing in the wind;
the severed hands of sycamores awash downriver
bereft of wrist or limb. Just where
in our faith or physics did we ever consider
what would come of this veined, green
benediction suspended above us all summer?

Sleepwalk

I've taken to walking my rooms at night.
I rise and weave through darkness safer than daylight,
when, rushing for doors or phones, I smack shins
against coffee tables.
                        By night, my thighs grow orchids;
my flesh burns with the clotted fire of stars; I pulse
thin colors as I glide through dangerous
familiar places.

                        I've taken to grinding my teeth nights.
Grit sifts from the sheets, drifts down the hall.
Daylight finds traces of my passing—white bonedust,
soft as ashes.
                        At dawn, my tongue smoothes
the only bones I can touch, gauging the depth
of night's erosion.

                        At this rate, I'll disappear
in something less than a lifetime,
flesh crushed by day, bones worn down by night
to powdered footprints
                        wandering
among the glass casters.

Presence

I. The terra cotta women

*after Mary Frank's sculptures**

I want to make . . .

    a woman in her solitude
    will cup and lift a breast: it is
    a negligent gesture, a human
    gravity
to make . . .

    a woman will wake, rocking,
    to the womb's throb, wake
    to concavity,
    time's hermetic cup
         I want to make . . .

      ❧

For the sketch, it's to our thinnest inks we turn,
   to the syntax of the wrist,
   to lift
     and quickened longing.
We take up brushes
when our need is for a thickness like ourselves:
     essential oils,
     the many salts; one way
     to keep the light inside *this world.*

But when we come to clays, it's for the commonness
and fossils,
   the muscles
of their hardening, the tastes
of their very names:

[70]

for *terra cotta, porcelain, raku;*
for the palate's changing pressure
on the consonant and vowel;
for *clay* itself:
laid flat on the farmer's tongue at dinner;
risen clear as cobble
   to the cantering horsewoman's ears;
   kindling the ancient cadence
   in the fire-and-brimstone preacher:
      Clay. We were clay, first,
      and He took us up . . . .

                    I want to make. . .

                    ✑

Her terra cotta women lie
in leaves. Fossil lines
      traverse their flesh.
            Women, these,
            of torn edges, abrupt breaks,
               hinges.
Women seasoned by earth's long stride,
inhabited by snakes
            and birds,
            their creases labial,
their layers draped and leavened,
lapped and caved
            upon themselves.

            Women, too,
of continuance,
wanting still to be wet, with leaves inside them;
      wanting, as well, to be air

[71]

                              reaching into elongation;
from there to the lift and loss
of dust.

                         I want to make . . .
                              ourselves.

This, the first of the long hungers.
There are others.

                          ❧

begin with the hunger to begin:
clay, to begin —
            begin with little,
enough to brim
the cup of your pressed palms.
                  press,
                  and place the wafer of it cold
                         on your tongue.

taste the many earths —
the basic salts and chromes,
burnt carbons, iron oxides,
            human sweat,
the bloods and bones
of bird and mammal young,
                  their beaks and horns and teeth,
the skulls of elders
buried in various skins and furs,
                  the bitter tang of droppings,
                  the leavings of earlier hungers —
                  seeds and lime.
taste, too, the spaces —

            the emptied basins of myriad grits,
            indentations and the air therein,
            the calligraphic hollows where
        small shells
        or spines have lain.
                and last,
the aftertastes —
of lightning, wood-ash, turf,
            the vast relentless rains
                    of stars and particles.

always, it has been a base
and savory earth.

color, next:
to sate this hunger, first, erase.
return to rarity — to blue.
                oh, the sky back then,
            the wet gemstone, the white
        spring hill;
        the cornflower
            and the wild rose;
        the oiled birds glistening after snow —
                and oh,
            the deep shades of bark
                and of burn;
                the many-muscled furs,
the browns and blacks, resplendent golds;
                        and all along,
the breaking down of weed and herb
to rot and stain;
            to pigment, then,
            and the first dyes drawn from the vegetable source

and *seen,*

                separate, uncontained—
                color *alone.*
then, slowly learned and slowly taught, the art
of the long dyes.
            vermilion, emerald, violet,
              the way flesh lit with the drape of it,
                the ways the human form
                  could move,
                    adorned.
oh, the colors that were, before colors turned
        to Barbiedoll pink, to awning green,
        turned *garish* and *hot,*
        turned *glow-in-the-dark*—

                oh, the *dark.*

and space:
a craving, a clenched longing
beyond naming,
            as if shoulders could ache
            with the lost weight of sky.
reach become a paltry thing;
        our elbows, an embarrassment;
            we watch our feet.
but here,
in the throat's hollow
        where we have embalmed gasp,
        here, we recall
        space:
        how once,
we filled our cells on the long light of distance
falling away into layer and lap,
            we fed

on cliff and sky,
on starlight (stardark),
on the distant linger or lift of birds,
the companionable passing of beasts, unseen;
we fed
on the uncontained.

and last, the need to deepen:
like the hunger of a river to channel, bed, and mouth; or
the hunger of the tongues of bells to carve their troughs in air; or
the hunger of shadows to burn the sundial stone.
the hunger of a lover for the deepening of love —
if only by a little,
the hunger to carve, by simply passing here,
a proper depth
for human passing,
for the bearing of a faith through the rock of a life.

this, the last of the hungers of clay:
by a little and a little,
the deepening of the heart.

⁂

A terra cotta woman
lies in leaf and fossil light.
One hand lifts a breast,
her fingers,
like the ridges of the oldest ranges,
splayed upon it.
Her eyes
have turned away into
a disconnect of such vast measure,

[75]

only her spine resists
a primal separation.
A woman prepared by earth and fire
to lie
through winter's long erasure of the heart.

All winter, she cups and lifts a breast
like an anguish, like a chalice;
all winter, she arches
the muscles of her throat,
strains
to raise her face beyond the possible, to speak—
a face
already so opened
she is past her voices.

I want to make . . .

II. A Face

after *Presence* by Mary Frank
"*I knew I would have to destroy the piece.*"

To reach the house you cross a creek on a wooden bridge. . .

    All stories begin with place,
    the path there. This one begins
             in the Catskills, begins
             with the terra cotta women
        whose nature it is
        to lie down —
            or fly.

          ❧

Ten years have passed since her daughter died
in the Amazon crash,
in the flames

      . . . and it's autumn again:
      azaleas, poppies, irises,
      black-eyed Susans, nasturtiums — all
             collapsed into rags, reduced
             and returned
             to the softened garden
        at Lake Hill House, where the story begins,
        where the kiln
        will not know fire till spring.

          ❧

Autumn now.
To reach the house . . .

            She has no wish to reach the house;

                    she has left the house
                    and the cold of the Catskills,
        left—with the last clay face unfinished,
        there, on the workbench:
                            one clay woman
        begun like others: shoulders and throat;
        the bones of a face;
                        eyes lowered, lips parted
                        to speak with the broken
                        strength of the stricken to heart;
                lips parted, yes, but the speaking
                stunned shut.

To reach the house . . .

                        this face has crossed
                        no bridge,
                        has taken no path.
        This face was born in the kiln house and found
        unworthy of fire.

        On the workbench, the face begins to reach
                        back into earth, out
                        into air
                                (to lie down—
                                        or fly)

                                   ❧

        Late autumn. No fire now in the lake house;
        well below freezing; the face has begun
        to crack open . . . but no,
                                more precisely,
                                cracks

                              open *in* her
                                    and move to the surface,
                                    open precisely where bone comes closest
                                    to skin (but she has no bone);
where flesh has thinned to assume the contours
of human beauty
                        (her beauty is not
                              human, it comes
                        of fingertips and thumbs, comes
                        of the pressed cup of the artist's palm.
                                          no bone, no flesh,
                                          only earth
                        abandoned here, and no fire now
                        till spring.)

Cracks cross the face through days
unbroken from nights, through nights
undivided by days.
                        The surface tightens, the eyelids thin
                        to admit thin light
                                    to the dark interior space on which
            the closed eyes fix. Her lips
            listen at the edge.
She is still.
And in her, the source of the stillness
moves.
            She dreams (if she dreams)
            as Demeter dreamed: of herself, returned
to a winter in which
she was always queen—and had no daughter.

                              ༺༻

                              [79]

All stories
begin with place, the path there.

Deep in winter
and safe in the city, the artist dreams of an early work,
her first *Moving Woman*, a figure
born from a fact (a photo. a nightmare.)
      a woman clothed in gasoline and set aflame;
     golden in gasoline, lit
             and fleeing.
A flesh-and-blood woman, from whose burning skin
a clay figure rose
       to fly in a nightmare beauty, to fly
       for ever (she is flying now,
except, in this dream, she is flying
          through jungle).
And now in the dream, the artist,
the mother,
     returns alone, she's crossing a bridge, a threshold, a floor
         to a face on a table, unbroken,
         a face she remembers leaving.
     The air
     is white in the dream, and hers
     is the only breath left.
       Even the snakes and mice
       have curled into sleep in their nests inside
       the reclining women,
         whose terra cotta beauty is fixed forever
         by fire; women
inhabited now all winter; women
who lie in the fields—
         or fly.

Late winter.
To reach the house now you would move
through hemlocks and mountain laurel,
move down the paths of the flower beds, move
over dead nasturtiums, dead cosmos,
          dead asters and lilies,
and boulders, the boulders, too, dead.

Spring. She returns.
The face on the workbench
          is broken so deeply it can't
          be mended, can't be fired,
and can't
                    (but why not? it's earth, only earth)
                    be destroyed.
(It must be destroyed.)

To reach a future mouth and eyes,
          you travel the cracks
          through spring and back in time across
          a winter's landscape of absence.

All spring she watches the cracks advance, reaching
toward eyes and mouth, the places a face gives
          itself away;
          where the face we were given
                    is first taken back;
          where at last we take back
                    ourselves.

[81]

Places of so deep a beauty,
we can't, we can't . . .
                    but she knows she must.

                    ❧

All stories begin with place, the cracks there.

Late summer.
The garden has grown so full, the kiln
casts a petaled shadow. Soon
            she will cast the face in a bronze so golden
            it might itself
            be flame.
                    (The beautiful, broken face,
                            unmended.)

The fissures will breathe and hold and be
the bone,
and soon the skin will burn with a sky patina,
and the face become
                    Presence:
                    the place all stories end.

iv.

"Many Mansions," by "his Father,"
I don't know him: snugly built!
Could the Children find their way there–
Some, would even trudge tonight!
                    –Emily Dickinson

Couplets for the Color Gold

Tonight straight down our street two planets square off against
that fat moon at my back and draw my heart in two.

If this kindness continues, unbearable, I will hide
myself, my love, in any arms but yours.

Once I loved tales of forest huts, woodcutters' virginal daughters.
Now I love paper in neat stacks, the smell of leaves illegally burning.

Far off armies train in the hills, but I think of your hands
and am glad enough to forget.

This year like all the others will depend on the fragile
limbs of lilac bushes. Still, no reason not to pray.

Leaves flatten and press themselves, transparent, into a plane of sun
already pouring with gold dustmotes, the broken shells of locusts.

Spills

For once,
      to prepare for the dark:
to take the salient fact, the sudden
crash of color
          or of storm—
one fact, wherever found, however hard;
to twist it up into a *spill*,
            the kind
a Dickens hero might have used
to light the walk down a dark hall
              to a darker cell,
to catch a torch for a deathwatch
or a dance;
      to store it in
a plain ceramic vase, against
a momentary draft or
            the solid dark.

But what I never understood
          is what one lit them on.
On another's flame?
On the chestnut-coals of vendors
         just outside one's door?
on fear? on stars?
What huge faith in fortuity, then!

And how to find that faith tonight
         and begin
the twisting up of expendable scraps
against the day when one slim wand,
           unfolding fast
and lasting only long enough to touch
tinder or wick,

                    might serve
in its singular burning to start
a hearthfire in an opened,
            brutal room of cold; or,
calming the heart when the last dark falls,
to illuminate in one's own palm
                    the revealed cup of bone.

What Cannot Be Summoned

Apples are easy, bruised to a soft
glistening there in the dust
of my grandmother's road to the schoolhouse;
easy, too, the grime-thick angels
etched in a two-thousand-year-old sky
above blurred shepherds beyond recognition;
even the milky birth of the first
vast spill we've cried over down the ages,
easy: dust and light.
                      But today's stars burning
beyond my glass and a million years off
in this overcast dawn before the birds,
they're harder. And birdsong,
harder still to command. It's terribly quiet.
My heart returns. And returns.

Unbidden, *the quick and the dead*
plies the pedal of some unnamable need,
sounding and muting itself at once
inside the bones of my skull and a million years off
where my spine remembers, or foresees,
absence; knows it for *cold.*
                      Unsummoned now,
a vision. Noon on a summer's road.
A shrew—tiny spilled thing:
fragile splay of ribs,
flung-satin drape of blood,
and three small bees dipping to feed
at the throat's break.
                    Impossible,
heart-stopping beauty: *white ladder;*
bright blood; a hovering, ivory
flight.
            Bow to it, bones of my neck, flesh
of my inner eye.

Mother of Lapse

The centuries have a way of being male.
                                        –Wallace Stevens

On the Baptistry doors, a late sun kindles
the smooth baby pate,
stirs the rougher shine of the saints,
deepens the folds of the mantle worn
by the one mother who matters
                to God.
In the singular moment before full dark,
three burnished skulls rise into light,
triangulating the holy family,
whose faces our abrasive lips
and acid thumbs have worn
                to gold.
Just see
what our fingers of flesh and salt
have done to bronze,
what the weight
of our mere waiting has done
                to stone—yes,
we're that lethal a substance.
Had we wished to escape
through prison walls,
we could have *licked* our way out by now,
but Time
                we can't erode,
those male centuries wheeling above us,
trailing the broken bloodlines of gods
and the mute herds of bullies and beasts
our eyes can slice
from any dark.

Intercede for us, Mother of lapse,
Mother of cast bronze,
           of stone,
Mother of all that can still succumb
                 to touch. To us.
Mother of touch, of tongue,
Mother of the Word's corrosive salt,
                       intercede for us.

❧

At the mouth of another of the long tunnels
   we've opened through mountains, I lift my eyes

to take in a high scatter of stars.
   Then stone closes in, and the sky's afterburn

on my retina turns suddenly wrong. In this high country,
   village lights cast themselves nightly off cliffs

into immortality—constellations
   rising from streets sliced through rock

as stubborn as the blocks Michelangelo carted
   down to the sea from the murderous slopes

of Carrara, where he quarried a stone
   already immortal—or at least, that white—

to render the flesh of the one mother
   with the grace to bear her unwieldy son

through a locked door. Huge burden, the family dead.
   And the missing, the driven-out, the fled.

At Chartres:
a woman on her knees with a bucket,
                              Mother
intoned in the rhythm of beads
tucked at her waist and swaying,
swaying,
          one flattened palm circling the blocks
          scrubbing the weight of our millions of feet
                              into the stone.
Stone shaped to a woman's knees. Stone
like a cup.

And the same Mother in an Alpine chapel,
where a scrap of paper penciled in German and left
on the virgin's altar
               asks only : *Maria,*
                         bring my sons back to the Hof.

And the same Mother of Repetition,
enshrined on mantels in simple homes
across three worlds;
               a woman
into whose wooden breasts a door has been cut
and rehung on a tiny hinge to open
                         a private place of petition.

And the mother whose face my fingers brush
again and again
          in the only photo I have left
that does not already contain
                    her death.

[91]

Straight up through the thick, unthinkable
stone of this tunnel,
clusters of villages cast constellations
into the sky
                from high stone streets,
                where supper is over and children
                                are rocked
                in the tongues of sleep, licking
their own way out, as always,
lullabied by women who sing
the prayer of milk and suck, the swaying prayer
                                of the work,
                                of the always, always undone.
The prayer of knees.
Of the Hof
                and the coming home of the sons; unaccountably home
                to stony farms, to villages cut
                out of rock and hung in a high dark
        where man can't dwell
                                short of being a hero.

                                Bring back, Maria, the sons.
                                The sons.

Always, the sons.

Imagine her face, her millions of faces,
kindled by love and leaning to hear,
age after age,
                the one prayer that matters
                                to *us.*

Imagine her turning in answer
to wheel back the stars and the suns of the decades—
a mother's work,
     so slight as to go
unnoticed in the circling of centuries.

And always, it's all we can think of to ask: *the sons,*
the sons,
          praying our long way back
          to an ancient space that once held the light
of a son still among us, who promised return
and can only return by turning again
into flesh, into time,
               into which is locked
the ancient dark we'll scar as before
with beasts and heroes,
               connecting the dots,
               beginning, as always, from death's lit skull
and drawing the elegant lines of the story
we can't escape: of return.

☙

It's a long tunnel through rock; at the far end
          the same old sky will collapse upon me,

a black, cup-shaped stone falling through time
          (as if Earth were the only mother who mattered)

toward this one globe—cold, lethal, and lit by nothing
          but our millennia of eyes turning up.

If our eyes were a less-watered salt,
          we'd have *looked* our way out by now.

Ste. Thérèsa's Small Wrist

My hunger's worn like modesty,
appeased in these small rooms
      in which I watch
my wrist bones at their white tilt
as I lift them toward lips
that are silent now—His.
My lips part and close
     over crusty softness,
my tongue cries water, and I am blessed.

This is not allegory, not euphemism:
we are not children here. This is Truth,
      the perfect hunger of my wish
to take to myself,
with the small watched gestures
of simple grace,
the bread of my sisters,
     baked in long kitchens
below these quiet cells.

We are not here for lost reasons
or doors closed before we remember.
      We are not saints. We love
this world's bread, its dark salt.
But beyond is the perfect
hunger
of the wrist to move slowly
     under lowered eyes,
to slim itself, turning,

into the white
transparence of light through
     a stone-cut window,

washing these planks that serve
as my desk,
and where bread is brought, sweet,
from down where my sisters
        are baking their silence
into the loaves.

Their goodness beckons my mouth's
still water,
            as I take a small piece
onto my tongue and
return to my pen.
Before I begin, I ask Him as always,
to allow me to carry
        for the little distance to the grave,
this perfect hunger, this

tiny thirst, only the size of my wrist
and His death.

Good Friday: On the Irish Coast

Dead bird on the rocks below,
rising and falling in a cup of stone.

Feathers mat the disproportionate
skull, a few cling wetly to what was throat.

For what reason on such a night,
against the winds, the odds,

that final going-nowhere-hard,
that brutal backward break onto vertical rock,

and the straight fall?
It's an unrepentant world—hard wind,

grim intermittent sun. Closer in,
gorse and hawthorn, twisted briar—

a hollowed place of ancient,
unremitting opposition. From the hills above,

where subsistence keeps its green and stony farms,
the lowing of a cow comes down

stunted, broken back in the lungs.
Here, or is it everywhere,

lives are singular, unadorned, reduced
to stubbornness or cling.

And soon enough, the breaking down.
The drowning of the traces.

Horizontal forces pin us to our lives. Safest
not to move against them.

◀❧▶

Here, on the rock outcroppings,
my shoes are only fingered by the sea,

a simple soak and leak of canvas, but
the sea's about to deepen, the frail bones below

be taken by the tide. A shadow moves
across the grasses and out over the lit bay.

My eyes follow it into the sudden
blot of black waters at the cliff base —

a shadow-gull, stunned to a shadow-death,
while the living flesh and sinew, presumably,

rise. Good Friday's proof of something
insisting on itself.

Not only a shadow's passing
into permanent dark

or the inhuman strength we would need
to shift one stone.

More like the horizontal drive
of nails through flesh. Or the thrust

that slams the wind from the lungs.
Death

by crucifixion, they say, is death
by suffocation,

a last breathtaking caesura
turned in the heart to stone. And then?

Whatever Easter's about, it's not about His rising,
that one-time-only lifting

of the hard ultimatum. Whatever it proves,
it denies Him a flesh

anything like our own. And so,
it's not about Love.

✣

If I stand on the last safe foothold,
open my arms to the horizontals

(the muscles of my calves tensed
to take it all back in an instant)

and, canted into peril, take the steady wind
onto both my palms. . . .

If . . . ,   then . . .

✣

Below, on the rocks, a hollow arc
rises and falls in a carved cup,

far beyond rescue or reach — immaculate
sockets, splayed bones, ribs emptier

than earth allows. If I let myself lean
into such a wind (if only an instant)

for such a thing. . . .
Christ, what must a cathedral mean?

. . . and are heavy laden

His watch begins after Tenebrae. All they ask
is he stay awake: the chalice wine, a *drug* now,

the kneelers' soft wood
and the Stations themselves, *good money.*

Every bronze nameplate, the pipes in the washroom,
the thick, warm banners that speak the Seasons—

someone here in his city knows
what they'll bring on the open market.

Only the bells are safe—too heavy to carry.
Still, the doors must stay open.

What he faces those first weeks is no one comes.
Worse, one Saturday deep into winter

a young woman comes, kneels for a time, and goes.
Then, for weeks, it's immensely silent.

Sometimes he stands outside the huge doors
gazing at stars or the stone moon.

Some of the streetlights
are dark.

And one night it forms—the thought
that's been coming to him all along:

he's the only one
awake—watching—in the whole city,

the only one who will ever come.

[100]

The Consistency of the Human

Each year, as leaves break from their branches,
a throng to bury the earth,
   I follow the chill air north,
praising the way the dying resist
the final *consistency* — call it *death*;
      call it less than that:
                dust.

             🙰

she is older now, closer.
in dreams, she wanders the catacombs, Belsen,
the banks of the Ganges;
      she's one of the multitudes, taking on
the human consistency.
         this time, it's Jesus.
she's barefoot in dust at the gates with the others.
he comes, her heart leaps, she thinks
      it will wake her.
she stills herself — wills her eyes lower.
not even a breath, not even so much
      as to catch a bit of the light
in her hair.
she's learning to draw no light to herself.
she's learning
    her death.

             🙰

And how many times must multiplicity
wash *my* feet in the hair
   of effacement,
my face into the ground
      of the given?

How long will it take to reduce and erase
even fear? even love?

How many more autumns of traveling north,
watching my heart break
        itself
from that knowledge?

Sacred Waters

The sun has only a short way to fall
behind the Italian Alps, but full
dark is a long time coming.
These endless evenings draw the ill
and elderly out
to stroll the gentle switchback trails
to the spa's high gardens.

I watch them at dinner, folding warm rolls
into their napkins,
capping the curative mineral water.
In the lift they are silent, formal,
holding the bottles as stiffly as vials
of mercury or urine samples.
Here, the waters are sacred;

they fall from the mountains like white
linen, sing in the distance all night,
and are precious. The rolls serve
another purpose:
beyond the first gate,
three hotel swans ply tended pools,
living on bread alone.

~❦~

Porcelain swans swam the glass
of my aunt's dining table: wings white as sun,
lifted, half-folded—a royal couple,
with holes at the spine
for dinner candles, whose fine, pale blades
curved with our breath, cutting, recutting
the mirrored ceiling.

Each endless Sunday
I longed to slam their glazed flesh down
on the porch cement.
Too old to believe in perfection—too old
and an ugly duckling—I knew
about lies and maintaining them,
while bread you were starving for fell

out of reach. Another of Sunday's
tedious lessons: grace before dinner,
polite conversation before dessert,
refolded napkins and hands, the long wait
before being excused.
Unmoving swans,
unmoving reflections of swans.

❧

Privileged, living on alms,
these swans no longer feel the cold
as a reason for wings. White as lies, they hold
the old pose, as though a porcelain child could curl
into the hollow at the spine. But
I've read Yeats, I know about rape,
about gods

who come down shining
in double-breasted suits,
offering love as their reason. Tonight,
I'll come down to the stone banks. There
in hollow light from the suites above,
where wakefulness and pain are real,
I'll catch them no longer *labouring*

to be beautiful, all beaks
and blinking yellow eyes, necks fat and slack,
reflections lapped by a murky tide.
I'll catch them picking at each other's flesh,
living, like us, on each other —
on something deep in each other, alive
and brutal at the skinline.

❧

The healing waters fall endlessly
from the high, formal gardens, but
only the dark is sacred.
In it, we remain unknown
even to our most ardent lovers
who swear they'll love us just the same
when beauty goes,

when even the hope of beauty goes.
In the lift tomorrow, they'll lean together,
the ill and the old,
whispering of greater miracles
in other mountains. When I enter,
they'll fall silent, holding their final voices
like flasks of sacred water.

v.

That there should be much goodness in the world,
Much kindness and intelligence, candor and charm,
And that it all goes down in the dust after a while,
This is a subject for the steadiest meditations
Of the heart and mind, as for the tears
That clarify the eye toward charity.

–Howard Nemerov

Invisible

I've learned to move in unfamiliar places
without sound. The old caretaker
who lifted one palm from the tractor wheel
to shade his eyes and smile
as I rattled up the drive
wonders now where I have got to:

upstairs

where the birds barely break their riff
as I open the balcony and step
into their sky. My step
is neither hesitant nor light.
In fact, I'm pronounced.
Heavy as all my bones put together. No,

tiptoe's not the trick.

Only mindful. Mindful
of the next stair suspended in the dark
in all its likely variance of level;
mindful of the fit
of keys, each one exact and
honorably intent

on opening, but only

when aligned inside its proper space;
mindful, too, of ownerships,
of overlapping lives I've crossed
in my best clothes—this cloak
of woven welcomes,
lifted hands, permissions.

Permission

the only given in this enterprise,
and all I ask
from the man behind the wheel,
the occupants
of rooms along these halls,
the birds at their lives.

Especially the birds.

Splendor

Wind wakes me,
          tantrum wind,
throwing its intransigent self every which way
and hard enough
          to set off the back security light.
Trees burst into turmoil, settle and hush,
then collapse again into all-out
panic.

I lie in the tanglings
          of lingering dream-stuff:
a princess phone dripping
on a gilt wire stand;
          lace curtains, drenched;
a random moon in storm clouds
wasting light; beside me,
a man,
          his black spine struck
          to a sudden white
by lightning—real? or cut from dream's
same bone?

I shiver in the mix,
          uncovered,
and let the chill run through me.
The next I know, I'm back,
          upright,
          in a tantrum dream:
a younger self,
window wide to a struck midnight,
white gauze standing
          straight out into my room.
Dripping sills, soaked floors—for these
I care nothing.

O *spacious skies*, you Westerner,
          you blow-hard boy,
splendor is a spent word. Here,
in the pent Mid-lands, we burn
          security: trees burglarize
our neighborhoods, our bushes
rampage, our grasses crush
the moon.

And all the time we lie, lit,
          in our sweet beds,
while around us the squandering wind
burns light,
          above us the *Splendid*
          storms.

Faith and the Heavy Machinery

I'm watching the graveyard for deer —
boring, I know, now that they're everywhere
over-running our lawns and malls, but
I think a person ought to watch
for something.
I'm watching for deer.

I think, too, no one's watching us here,
what with infinite space, so little light,
and matter tossed loose as the dirt
they mound on these graves
to await the arrival
of the heavy machinery.

Do they still use water drums for the rolling?
I hope so. An elegant substance, water,
its weight a surprising extra. Later,
the earth will sink a bit at the site.
It's ourselves, I think,
tucking ourselves in.

Next week or the next: fresh dirt;
then, to tamp down the seams, the drums return
containing, most likely, the same water.
A little older, if water ages.
Wiser,
if water learns.

Perhaps, a more cynical water next time,
beginning to know what it does for a living,
beginning to wish it could just start over,
return to the river —
reflect a bit. Sing.
Flow faster downstream next time around.

Manna

Swallows slice low across the field, feeding
                                on the unseen.
Deep in their two-hundred-million-year birdness,
they know precisely what they're doing.
But briefly,
            it strikes me as sad
that they don't know how lovely they are
to watch,
        how rare in this world, such accuracy.

My husband, the agnostic, interrupts
to read from *The Bible As History*:
manna —
a secretion of tamarisk bushes pierced
                                by a plant louse,
and shows me a photo of crystallized honey,
white when it falls, then turning yellow.
If it's not collected each morning, he adds,
            the ants take it.

I guess I prefer those who believe
                        in small things,
keeping their large disbeliefs to themselves,
though I like them mostly
for their quiet entry into a room
        with an odd bit of knowledge,
        the way they'll wait for the right moment
        to offer
                the weight of a songbird's blood,
                the stomach contents of the dead pharaohs,
                the titles of books thought to have burned
                        in the Alexandria library.

Even if what they bring you is only the ball score,
or the fact that they've seen the egret again
                              out on the Interstate,
mostly they're willing to wait a bit
        if you're watching the swallows.

Poem in Which Krishna Appears As Heron

Lifting awkwardly, scattering beaded droplets to pocket
    the lake's pearl surface,

a heron not thirty feet from my door. Wings. White.
    My heart startled,

my flat palm pressed against air where the door swung away.
    And the replay: my entry,

blear-eyed, into another chilled dawn; the draw of my breath
    at the starched unfolding;

the muted crumple of space when the heron walked
    into air.

Once, driving fast in broad day, a deer—huge,
    in space and time's

drawn bead. The swerve and burn of tires, and for
    long minutes after,

the race of two hearts escaping one another. Does this
    sound like love to you?

❧

The young immortals on their jet skis slice each other's wakes
    in tightening curves

and disappear, heading, may it be, for home docks, as lightning
    scores the sky.

Here in my doorway, I pray the storm in. Wind
    bellies the screens,

[116]

sieving the ozoned air. Krishna called memory *smrti* — not,
    as I've always thought,

the linear tracings of one's own past, but the calling forth
    of latent impressions

left by those rare events that transcend our personal lives.
    Love, again?

꧁꧂

Down across the lake sweeps a bodied wind. The lake-skin
    tarnishes in streaks

of black; the sky purls white: a second coming of the crazed
    wake-cutting of the wild

young men. Improbable, this duplication — but a heron has come
    to feed at my shallows;

I know the translation of a god when I see one.
    Sleep, Krishna tells me.

Sleep, and this will stay — in the rafters, in the sand.
    Sleep, and it will come again

with something of the hollow of your grave
    in its return.

꧁꧂

Uniformly beaded now, my screen suggests a universe
    of pearls

reflecting pearls, in one of which a heron stands, feeding,
ankle-deep in me;

a young doe, improbable, settles in the leaves. May these
impress the darkness

May the lake's soft pocketing last all night, as though
a curtain

of herons were forever rising. May the blown sound
of thunder and

the imprint of birdcall recur. May my heart lift awkwardly
—like love?

to bear their crossing, my memory of them latent in
their memory of me.

Sunburn Song

Skinflint morning,
sing me a song
of stockpiled shadow
in deep canyon lands,
a song to remind me:
what the world blocks,
it blocks.

Navajo sandstone,
powdering down
to the skinny river,
sing me a song
of metric tons moving
over eons
and seasons.

Mid-morning sun,
riding shallow
in the riffled pebble-bed,
sing me a Calvinistic
tributary song,
sing me the hydro-
electric ripple.

And just downhill
from the prickly pear,
where the sacred datura
unfolded her silks
at first light, already
her petals lie limp
from tonguing the sun.
Sing me her song.

Noonday. Noonday.
Sing me the rush
of downhill water
from upstream pools,
sing me of liquified
sun on pinyon
and aspen too sated
on gold to quake.

Sing me the song
of *silk* turned *sulk*,
of *stuporous* sinking
to *rash*, of *rush*
turned *rampant*,
and turned away
into pools of *sidelined*
and *stagnant*.

Sing me
the downhill slide
of the day:
the mind-eroding song
of the won't-shut-up-bird,
of yucca after yucca,
of the creosote burning,
sing me:
creeee–oh — sote,
creeee–oh — sote,
creeee–oh — sote,

and let sunscreen block
what sunscreen
blocks: death,

if I'm lucky–
luck blocking only
luck. So.
Sing me your best
living-lucky song,
and shadow me a shadow,
creosote bush.

And you,
thin-leaved yucca,
bulk out and bully
my shadow-shape
with yours
on this hot rock,
and let the world block
what the world
can block. (Bad luck,
if I'm lucky.)

The ants keep on
sinking into sand
racing and balking
refraining and refraining
in a huge sinking world,
just singing along
on their hardwired
way and all ways
blocked, so . . .

sing me a song with
a theme and variation.
Re-navigation.
Re-calibration.

Sing of innovation,
—the waffle-weave
of jeans,
of their mystifying
place in the ants'
Great Work.

Sing a workday song
of the carrying out
of carrying back,
of burden and boredom,
of the on-going, flat-out
lichening of light and
the same old drill
of thirsting roots
thrusting down
through sand
through stone,
and the canyon wren
on break again
shooting the breeze
by the cooler waters,

while clouds, in
out of the blue,
pass vaguely-
worded memos
from other departments,
but you can't
make them out,
couldn't find a camel,
not the vaguest uncle
of a face, 'cause

it's all in flux.
Well,
transitions
and hard times
are difficult to whistle,
and the sky's no help,
just humming along,
idly idly,
just kicking rocks
to no great purpose.

So sing me a wind song,
any old wind song:
zephyr; wisp.
Just sing me
anything.
Anything helps.
Sing me the creosote
song again,
add in the scrub—
the *scrub scrub scrub*.
Add
a canyon-wren coda,
a canyon-oak reprise.

Now sing me
a late-in-the-day
light song,
of long-faced shadows,
captive, canyon-locked.
Lullaby me now,
you know it's time,
rock me by, baby.
Sing it once again:

the siltstone,
the blue-blooded,
thin-veined datura,
the sandstone
and aspen, rocks
underwater, rocks
in the sun. Sing me
the old anty-song,
Goin' Home,
but sing it like a pro.

Sing me down
to darkness
with that lucky-ol' sun,
that baby-will-fall,
lethal burn-
of-a-sun.
Let me blaze,
sunset-colored,
in this cradle-of-rock,
and let the world
block
what the world will block.

Tourist

If she could sit like stone
on this stone ledge,
steep wind tearing

her hair back, knees
sealed to clavicle, shins
in a tight forearm-grip —

a paperclip of flesh —
how long
would leaving take?

Her breath would slow
to nearly nothing. Her heart, as well.
Her arms would loosen,

open. Her heat
would dissipate,
and with it, words:

storm-clouds, solitude,
sit like stone,
the failed instruction,

rise:
use every trace of
everything you have

to rise.
If she could sit
past *rise* —

Birds would venture in
to carry off her flesh,
the threads of rotting cloth.

In time
her stone-colored bones,
unfolded, would lie

beyond the hungers, lie
where other lives
had moved them;

would polish, powder,
sift into
the elements;

would chase
the four directions down;
would wheel within wheels, pass

through the fire-flash of days
and out
onto night's plains:

day on night, black ice
on wing, shadow on mandible,
carapace on seed;

through settle, to toss,
to rest again—arrived
in the gaze

of all the gazes—
life-sized and
other-wise.

Autumnal

I climbed the field at dusk
  to breathe the sweep and height,

to feel my skin lift, as if
  in practice for an afterlife

in a sky like this—so immense
  I could fold it like a sheet,

but only if everyone I ever loved
  took up an arms' reach.

If they all came back.
  If I meant that much.

Prayer

Watch,
as breath slips its gradient
into and out of
a slanted awareness:
the pause at the base that says *next*
(and terrifies) and *must*.

Outside,
all those seeds wanting—
only wanting—in all those fields
and lots and cracks of the abandoned, wanting
what *we* want
and *that hard* in all directions
as a child wants, crying

up and down
as if flesh could crack open and this hurt,
this hunger, could hook into something
that will end in bigger
or in bloom
and lodge there,

wanting
only the *next* thing, the thing
beyond
that is so mad a hunger
we call it

for god
call it endlessly
nameless and thinner
than nameless, and more
and more fiercely,

calling
as if we'll crack open of pure

    wanting
and meaning
will bloom out in all
directions, true, and the answer,
and no
next thing will occur (like a terror)
to us ever

    amen.

Notes

Cover: Photograph by Alfred Böschl, "House on the Salt," from his Salt Flats series, Utah, 2000. Reproduced by permission of the artist.

Page 1: "What I Want To Say" by Mona Van Duyn from *To See, To Take*, (New York: Atheneum, 1973).

Page 4: The quoted phrase is from a review in the *St. Louis Post-Dispatch*.

Page 21: "The Layers." Copyright © 1978 by Stanley Kunitz, from *Passing Through: The Later Poems New and Selected* by Stanley Kunitz. Used by permission of W. W. Norton & Company, Inc.

Page 33: The Spurling quote appeared in the *St. Louis Post-Dispatch*.

Page 41: The opening reference is to lines, loosely quoted, from "Baggot Street Deserta" by Thomas Kinsella, 1961.

Pages 44-51: Epigraphs are from Robert Firmage's "Translator's Introduction" to *Song of the West: Selected Poems of Georg Trakl* (San Francisco: North Point Press, 1988).

Page 53: "On the Shingle" by Donald Finkel from *A Question of Seeing* (Fayetteville: University of Arkansas Press, 1998).

Pages 61-65: Italicized sections in this poem are taken from the entry on "medicine" in the 1771 edition of the *Encyclopedia Britannica*.

Page 66: "As If the Dark Were a Wind" first appeared in *Sow's Ear Review* under the title "Wind at the Glass."

Page 70: *Presence* by Mary Frank, a bronze sculpture with blue patina, is housed now in the Harvard Graduate School of Business Administration. Works in Frank's powerful series of archetypal ceramic, plaster, and terra cotta sculptures of women, some of which remain on the grounds of her studio in the Catskills, became more jagged, distorted, fragmented after the death of her twenty-year-old daughter in a plane crash in the Guatemalan jungle. The epigraphs for this poem are taken from Hayden Herrera's *Mary Frank* (New York: Harry N. Abrams, 1990) and used by permission of the publisher.

Page 83: Emily Dickinson: #127 ("Houses"—so the Wise Men tell me—) from *The Complete Poems of Emily Dickinson*, Thomas H. Johnson, ed., (Boston: Little, Brown, and Company, 1951).

Page 89: The epigraph comes from Wallace Stevens's essay "The Figure of the Youth as Virile Poet" in *The Necessary Angel* (New York: Vintage Books, Random House, 1951).

Page 94: The title refers to Thérèsa de Lisieux (1873-97), the French Carmelite nun, also called the "Little Flower of Jesus."

Page 104: The allusion is to William Butler Yeats's "Leda and the Swan;" the quoted line ("labouring to be beautiful") is taken from Yeats's "Adam's Curse."

Page 108: Howard Nemerov, "The Painter Dreaming in the Scholar's House" from *The Collected Poems of Howard Nemerov* (Chicago: University of Chicago Press, 1977 and originally published in *Gnomes & Occasions* (Chicago: University of Chicago Press, 1973) and included here by permission of Margaret Nemerov.

Acknowledgments

For the generosity of their instruction and encouragement, I wish to thank my teachers at Washington University in St. Louis—Donald Finkel, Mona Van Duyn, and Howard Nemerov—whose words can be found on the divider pages of this book.

I am indebted to the Virginia Center for the Creative Arts, whose fellowships provided the time, space, and nurturing environment in which a number of these poems saw their beginnings.

Sincere thanks to Alfred Böschl for offering the use of his site-sculpture "House on the Salt" for the cover of this book.

Acknowledgement and thanks to the editors of the following publications in which some of the poems in this book first appeared: *American Literary Review*, "Good Friday: On the Irish Coast"; *Bellingham Review*, "Baptism"; *The Cape Rock*: "Miniature on the Irish Ferry" & "Preservation"; *The Chariton Review*: "A Heart" & "These Hands Only"; *Chelsea*: "Couplets for the Color Gold, " "Berlin: Spring Equinox" & "At the Czech Border"; *Elixir*: "In this shot"; *The Florida Review*: "Manna"; *Gardening the Sky—1st Missouri Writers Biennial Awards Volume*: "Sleepwalk"; *The Journal*: "Prayer"; *The Iowa Review*: "Tourist"; *Kestral*: "Chestnuts"; *The Kenyon Review*: "Sacred Waters"; *The Lullwater Review*: "Graduation"; *The Malahat Review*: "The Tower"; *The Midwest Quarterly*: "Spills"; *Natural Bridge*: "Splendor"; *New Letters*: "What Cannot Be Summoned"; *New Orleans Review*: "Insurgence"; *Poet Lore*: "Autumn"; *Prairie Schooner*: "Poem in Which Krishna Appears As Heron"; *River Styx*: "Deathbed Confession," "Diseases of the Night" & "Faith and the Heavy Machinery"; *Southern Poetry Review*: "In a Finite Atmosphere"; *Sou'wester*: "Ste. Thérèsa's Small Wrist"; *The Sow's Ear Poetry Review*: "Autumnal" & " Wind at the Glass"; *The Spoon River Review*: "Sunburn Song"; *Tampa Review*: "The Middle Spaces" & "Radium"; and *The William & Mary Review*: ". . . and are heavy laden." Thanks also to Basilisk Press, which published *Presence* in their chapbook series, 2003, and to A.C.U. Press, which reprinted "Manna" in *Shadow & Light: Literature and the Life of Faith*, Darryl Tippens, Stephen Weathers, and Jeanne Murray Walker, eds., 2005.

Finally, I am especially grateful to Richard Mathews, editor and director at the University of Tampa Press, for bringing this book into being with, in Howard Nemerov's words, "much kindness and intelligence, candor and charm."

About the Author and Artist

Marjorie Stelmach received the Marianne Moore Poetry Prize for her first book, *Night Drawings*, published in 1995 by Helicon Nine Editions. A long-time resident of St. Louis, she taught in the public schools there for three decades, taking a sabbatical to earn an MFA from Washington University. Her poetry has appeared widely in journals including *Chelsea, Iowa Review, Kenyon Review, Midwest Quarterly, New Letters, Poet Lore, Prairie Schooner, River Styx, Southern Poetry Review,* and *Tampa Review*. She currently directs the Howard Nemerov Writing Scholars Program at Washington University in St. Louis.

Alfred Böschl is a Bavarian artist whose works are widely displayed and internationally known. His many awards include the 1994 Regensburg Culture Prize and the prestigious *Verleihung des Bundesverdienstkreuzes* for his contributions to German culture. His body of work embraces all aspects of sacred art—including stained glass, bronze sculpture, altarpieces, fountains, and chapel designs—as well as public sculptures, performance art, and photography. The cover photo, featuring his trademark *"Haus,"* is taken from a series begun in 2000 constructed on the Salt Flats in Utah. He lives in Adlhausen, Germany.

About the Book

A *History of Disappearance* is set in Electra types designed by the American artist and illustrator William A. Dwiggins in 1935. In this font, Dwiggins combines modern machine-age style with the flavor of hand-written letterforms to achieve an original new typeface of subtle warmth and grace. As Dwiggins explained, "if you don't get your type warm it will be just a smooth, commonplace, third-rate piece of good machine technique, no use at all for setting down warm human ideas, just a box full of rivets. . . . I'd like to make it warm, so full of blood and personality that it would jump at you." The book was designed and typeset by Richard Mathews at the University of Tampa Press.

POETRY FROM THE UNIVERSITY OF TAMPA PRESS

Jenny Browne, *At Once*

Richard Chess, *Chair in the Desert*

Richard Chess, *Tekiah*

Jane Ellen Glasser, *Light Persists**

Kathleen Jesme, *Fire Eater*

Lance Larsen, *In All Their Animal Brilliance**

Julia B. Levine, *Ask**

Sarah Maclay, *Whore**

John Willis Menard, *Lays in Summer Lands*

Jordan Smith, *For Appearances**

Jordan Smith, *The Names of Things Are Leaving*

Lisa M. Steinman, *Carslaw's Sequences*

Marjorie Stelmach, *A History of Disappearance*

Richard Terrill, *Coming Late to Rachmaninoff*

Matt Yurdana, *Public Gestures*

* *Denotes winner of the Tampa Review Prize for Poetry*